THEMATIC UNIT
Frogs and Toads

Written by Wendy Conklin

Teacher Created Materials, Inc.
6421 Industry Way
Westminster, CA 92683
www.teachercreated.com

©2001 Teacher Created Materials, Inc.
Reprinted, 2003
Made in U.S.A.

ISBN-0-7439-3086-X

Edited by
Gisela Lee

Illustrated by

D1300601

Table of Contents

Introduction

Frogs and Toads is a fun-filled, 80-page thematic unit designed to immerse children in writing, poetry, language arts, science, math, social studies, music, and art. The literature and activities used in this thematic unit have been selected to help children gain a better understanding about frogs and toads. In addition, children will experience working cooperatively, being considerate of others, and taking into consideration another's point of view. A variety of teaching strategies such as cooperative learning, hands-on experiences, and child-centered assessment are integrated throughout the unit.

This thematic unit includes the following:

❏ **literature selections**—summaries of three children's books with related lessons (complete with reproducible pages) that cross the curriculum

❏ **writing experiences**—suggested selections and lessons enabling children to write and publish their own works

❏ **planning guides**—suggestions for sequencing lessons each day of the unit

❏ **bulletin board ideas**—suggestions and plans for child-created and/or interactive bulletin boards

❏ **curriculum connections**—activities in language arts, math, science, social studies, art, and music

❏ **culminating activities**—projects which require children to synthesize their learning to produce products and engage in activities that can be shared with others

❏ **an annotated bibliography**—suggestions for additional literature and nonfiction books on the theme

> To keep this valuable resource intact so that it can be used year after year, you may wish to punch holes in the pages and store them in a three-ring binder.

Introduction *(cont.)*

Why a Balanced Approach?

The strength of a whole language approach is that it involves children in using many modes of communication: reading, writing, listening, illustrating, and doing. Communication skills are interconnected and integrated into lessons that emphasize the whole of language. Balancing this approach is our knowledge that every whole—including individual words—is composed of parts, and directed study of those parts can help a child to master the whole. Experience and research tell us that regular attention to phonics, other word-attack skills, spelling, and so forth, develop reading mastery, thereby fulfilling the unity of the whole-language experience. The child is thus led to read, write, spell, speak, and listen confidently in response to a literature experience introduced by the teacher. In these ways, language skills grow rapidly, stimulated by direct practice, involvement, and interest in the topic at hand.

Why Thematic Planning?

One very useful tool for implementing a balanced language program is thematic planning. By choosing a theme with correlating literature selections for a unit of study, a teacher can plan activities throughout the day that lead to a cohesive, in-depth study of the topic. Children will be practicing and applying their skills in meaningful contexts. Consequently, they tend to learn and retain more. Both teachers and children will be freed from a day that is broken into unrelated segments of isolated drill and practice.

Why Cooperative Learning?

Besides academic skills and content, children need to learn social skills. No longer can this area of development be taken for granted. Children must learn to work cooperatively in groups in order to function well in modern society. Group activities should be a regular part of school life, and teachers should consciously include social objectives as well as academic objectives in their planning. For example, a group working together to write a report may need to select a leader. The teacher should make clear to the children the qualities of good leader-follower group interactions and monitor them, just as he or she would state and monitor the academic goals of the project.

Why Journals?

Each day your children should have the opportunity to write in a journal. They may respond to a book or an event in history, write about a personal experience, or answer a general "question of the day" posed by the teacher. The cumulative journal provides an excellent means of documenting children's writing progress.

Frog and Toad Are Friends

by Arnold Lobel

Summary

Frog and Toad Are Friends *tells a wonderful story about two friends who experience daily struggles together and try to solve problems. Whether it is locating a missing button, taking care of each other when they are sick, or writing letters so they won't be lonely, these two friends bring out the best in each other.*

Students can be led by the teacher in problem-solving activities as they encounter each chapter. Below is a five-day sample plan that can be adapted to the classroom's needs.

Sample Plan

Lesson 1

- Discuss the information about frogs and toads (page 8).
- Read chapter 1.
- Research A Calendar of Holidays (page 11).
- Find a new home for Frog and Toad (page 9).
- Make spring trees (page 10).

Lesson 2

- Read chapter 2.
- Write a story using the story starters on page 12.
- Play Frog and Toad Scrabble (page 13).
- Make a Frog and Toad Venn diagram (page 64).

Lesson 3

- Read chapter 3.
- Practice math with Buttons, Buttons Everywhere (page 14).
- Design a jacket for Frog (page 15).

- Create puppets for a Frog and Toad Puppet Show (page 21).

Lesson 4

- Read chapter 4.
- Help improve Toad's swimsuit (page 16).
- Write safety rules for swimming (page 17).
- Practice math with Frog Leg Measuring (pages 58 and 59).
- Write some Frog and Toad poetry (page 49).

Lesson 5

- Write a letter for Toad (pages 18 and 19).
- Place a want ad for a friend (page 20).
- Find Frog Facts (page 56).
- Perform a puppet show for all to enjoy (page 21).

Overview of Activities

Setting the Stage

1. Prepare and assemble some or all of the Setting the Stage resources.

   - *Tadpole Observation Station*: Create your own tadpole observation station in an area of the room. See page 63 for instructions.

   - *Pond Reading Center*: Set up a pond reading center in a corner of the room. Beanbag chairs or large pillows can be the lily pads that students can read upon, and stones can mark the edge of the pond. Students can bring in stuffed animals (birds, snakes, lizards, mice, insects, frogs, etc.). Draw a pond on butcher paper and use it as a beautiful backdrop. Refer to the Annotated Bibliography (pages 78 and 79) for a list of books about frogs and toads.

   - *Multimedia*: Preview all videos and cassette recordings (see page 77) so you know which selections will work best for your class.

2. Ask students to explain what a frog is and what a toad is. Ask students if they know about the similarities and differences between them. Share some information from About Frogs and Toads on page 8 with your students to get them interested and excited.

3. Introduce the book *Frog and Toad Are Friends* and ask what students think the story is about based on its cover. Ask the class to explain what it means to be a friend. Read the book—a chapter a day for five days—aloud with your class.

Enjoying the Book

1. After reading and discussing the first chapter and using old calendars, have students complete A Calendar of Holidays (page 11), explaining the holidays that Toad misses every year because he is sleeping. Students are to write their opinions about these holidays. Then let students' creativity soar with A New Home (page 9) and A Spring Tree (page 10). For the new home activity, students will use magazines, newspapers, posters, etc., to find a new home for Frog. Use sources in the bibliography to help students, if needed. Some students might say a spaceship, a log cabin, or a boat. This makes a great bulletin board with lily pad explanations as the border and the picture collage in the middle. Before students begin making their spring trees, have a class discussion about what happens during (and topics related to) spring. When students make their spring trees, they can be as creative as they want.

2. The following day, read chapter 2 and discuss it. Students should then try to write a story to tell Frog, using the Story Starters for Toad (page 12). These story starters are optional. Students are also encouraged to write other story starters for Toad in case he has a difficult time thinking of another story for Frog. The Frog and Toad Scrabble (page 13) is a great spelling activity. Have students cut out the squares and arrange the squares into new words. Have a contest to see how many words your class can find. To keep track of how many they find, have students write the words that they spell on a separate sheet of paper.

Overview of Activities *(cont.)*

Enjoying the Book (cont.)

3. After reading chapter 3, distribute buttons to students. These buttons can be donated by parents, faculty, etc. Have students work on Buttons, Buttons Everywhere (page 14) using the buttons as manipulatives. Students can use the buttons as counters to solve the problems. Then students can make A Jacket for Frog (page 15). Copy this page onto tagboard so that it is sturdy enough to hold the glued buttons. Students can decorate the jacket with glitter, crayons, markers, sequins, etc., and then glue buttons to resemble the buttons that Toad found for his jacket. Students will also need to begin creating puppets (page 21) for the puppet show.

4. Read chapter 4 and discuss it. Have students redesign Toad's swimsuit (page 16). They can add to or take away from the swimsuit to make it less embarrassing for Toad. Then students can talk about swimming safety as well as the different types of swimming strokes and how to jump into a pool. On the template of a lifesaver (page 17), have students write directions to a frog who cannot swim. It can be about how to swim, swimming safety instructions, how to do the backstroke or the dog paddle. After students have written their instructions and cut out their templates, they can decorate their lifesavers. Display these lifesavers in the hallway strung with rope. This is also the day that students will need to practice for their Frog and Toad Puppet Show (page 21).

5. Read and discuss chapter 5. Students can then work on writing friendly letters and addressing envelopes (pages 18 and 19). Make sure that they have an envelope to address as well. Wanted: A Good Friend (page 20) gives the students practice in thinking of adjectives. Bring in want ads from the local newspaper to use as examples. Brainstorm as a class first, then let students write their own want ads. Since this is the last day of *Frog and Toad Are Friends*, students will be performing their puppet shows.

Extending the Book

1. Students will learn about the life cycle of an amphibian. Have students complete the Life Cycle of an Amphibian (page 66). Begin the Tadpole Observation Station (page 63) and ask students to write daily observations about what they see.

2. As students learn the differences between a frog and toad, they can complete the Venn diagram (page 64). Use sources in the bibliography. This can also be done on a bulletin board, using hula hoops for the Venn diagram. Students can place descriptive index cards inside the hula hoops. Have students work in groups to research.

3. After students read about the different seasons of the pond (page 61), have a class discussion about the different seasons. After the discussion, have students answer the comprehension questions (page 62).

4. Students can complete the writing activity, Frog and Toad Poetry (page 49), where students write a diamante poem about opposites.

5. Students will enjoy Frog Leg Measuring (pages 58 and 59) and Frog Facts (page 56) which will also extend math practice.

About Frogs and Toads

Teacher Note: On this page you will find some important facts for your own reference, written with simple explanations so you can share these facts with your students.

- Frogs have two sets of eyelids on each eye. Underwater, the frog closes the second eyelid, which is clear, to protect its eyes from the water.

- In the spring, a female frog makes thousands of eggs which are fertilized with sperm from the male frog. The male frog attracts the female frog by expanding his vocal cords and making a croaking noise. Different species of frogs and toads have different mating calls. This enables a female to find her own species to mate with.

- Amphibians breathe underwater when they are first born. Later, they develop lungs to breathe air on land. This change is called metamorphosis.

- Both frogs and toads are cold-blooded animals and depend on their surroundings to regulate their body temperatures.

- It is possible for frogs and toads to reach their full size within one year.

- Frogs and toads can live up to 20 years. One toad lived for 36 years.

- Frogs and toads drink water through their skin instead of their mouth.

- Frogs and toads will only eat food that is alive. They ignore dead insects.

- Frogs and toads hibernate all winter in burrows. While in this sleep state, their breathing slows, and they live off the fat of their bodies for the next few months.

- There is a tree frog in Japan that never lives in water. The eggs are laid in foam (produced from the parents) on the ground. The foam is soft and liquidy on the inside, but hard on the outside. The tadpoles hatch inside the foam and develop into young frogs.

- A frog's tongue is fastened at the front of his mouth (instead of at the back) so that it can easily snag its supper.

A New Home

Directions: Frog and Toad both live in houses. Scientists tell us that frogs need to live near water because their skin needs moisture. Toads don't have to live in water because a toad's skin can hold moisture better than a frog's skin. But if frogs and toads could live anywhere, where would you have them live? Using magazines and newspapers, cut out pictures and paste them on paper to create a collage of ideal living places for a frog and a toad. On the lily pad below (which can act as a border for the collage), write why the frog or toad would like his new home better than a pond.

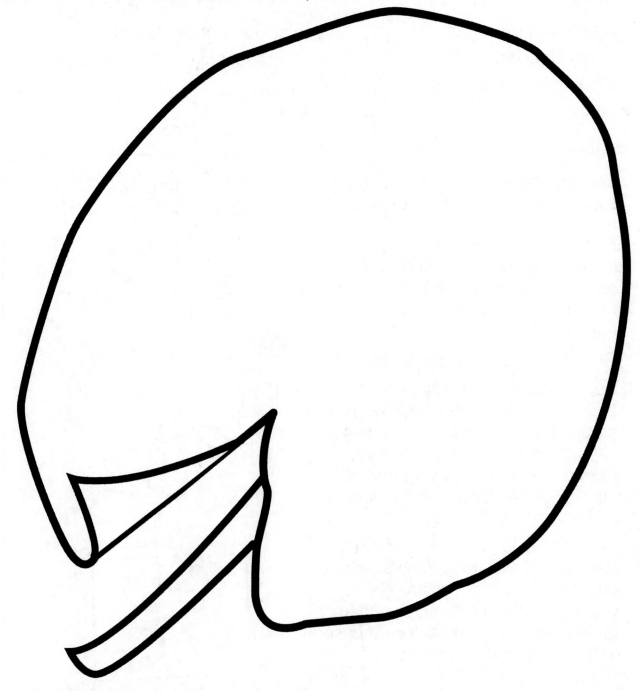

A Spring Tree

Teacher Note: *The teacher may need to pre-cut the tissue paper and use a pencil to form little blossoms from the pre-cut pieces so children can use them to make their spring trees.*

Trees come to life in the spring, forming buds and leaves. Some trees flower beautifully and add dainty pastel colors to the spring landscape.

Directions: Make a spring tree by following the directions below. Keep the tree to decorate your desk or classroom bulletin board or give it to a friend or relative.

Materials

- brown chenille sticks
- green floral tape
- tissue paper (green, pink, purple, or yellow)
- small piece of cardboard
- white sheet of construction paper
- scissors
- glue

Directions

1. Use six chenille sticks and twist the six pieces together gently to form the trunk, leaving about 2–4 inches (5–10 cm) unwound at the top and bottom. Spread the bottom wires apart to form the roots and then bend the top wires of your tree to look like real branches.

2. Glue the roots to the cardboard.

3. Cut the tissue paper into 1-inch (2.5-cm) squares. Press each tissue around the eraser part of your pencil to form a little blossom. Wrap the base of the blossom with green floral tape. Glue the blossoms and leaves to the tree branches.

4. Draw and color springtime animals like birds, toads, frogs, rabbits, etc., on a white sheet of construction paper. Cut them out and glue them on the tree or on the cardboard base to decorate your spring tree.

A Calendar of Holidays

Directions: Frog tore off Toad's calendar pages from November to April. Toad had slept all those months and missed many holidays. Using a calendar, find out what holidays Toad missed. If some of those holidays are shown in any of the pictures below, cut them out and glue each picture on a separate 5" x 8" (13 cm x 20 cm) index card. Below each holiday picture that you cut out, write three or four sentences on the index card. Make a holiday mini book by stapling your index cards together. (Optional: You may also color the pictures in your mini book and/or add a cover to it.)

Story Starters for Toad

Toad had a hard time thinking of a story to tell Frog. Toad could have used these story starters below for help. If you were Toad, what story would you have told to Frog?

Directions: Use one story starter below to write a story for Frog.

It all began when Frog left the door open . . .
Toad was enjoying his lunch when all of a sudden . . .
Last night Frog had a dream . . .
Everything was quiet at the pond until . . .

_____

_____

_____

_____

_____

_____

_____

_____

Challenge: Can you think of some more story starters to add to the list for Toad?

12

Frog and Toad Scrabble

Directions: Cut out the squares below to use in a spelling game. Arrange the squares to create words. How many words can you make? **Bonus:** Can you find any five letter words?

F	R	O
G	A	N
D	T	O
A	D	

Buttons, Buttons Everywhere

Directions: Draw the correct number of buttons in each box. Use some buttons as manipulatives to solve the word problems below.

1. Frog had 3 buttons. Toad had 4 buttons. How many buttons did they have all together?

Frog's buttons	+	Toad's buttons	=	total

2. How many more buttons does Toad have than Frog?

Toad's buttons	–	Frog's buttons	=	difference

3. Toad had 4 buttons on his jacket. He found a black colored one, one button with two holes, one small button, one square button, and one thin button and put them in his pocket. How many buttons did he have all together?

buttons on Toad's jacket	+	buttons Toad found	=	total

4. Toad also found his original button. How many buttons did Toad sew onto his jacket?

buttons Toad found	+	Toad's original button	=	total

5. Then how many buttons did Toad have all together on his jacket?

buttons already on jacket	+	buttons sewed	=	total number of buttons on jacket

A Jacket for Frog

Teacher Note: *The template provided below may need to be enlarged when copied.*

Because Frog tried to help Toad find his button, Toad decided to give his jacket to Frog as a gift.

Directions: Decorate and glue buttons on the jacket below to give as a gift to Frog. Try to find a black button, a two-hole button, a small button, a square button, and a thin button, as well as five other buttons to decorate the jacket.

Help for an Embarrassing Swimsuit

Directions: Toad was embarrassed about his swimsuit, and you, a creative clothing designer, must help Toad with this problem. Since Toad doesn't have any money to buy a new swimsuit, in what ways might you help Toad to improve his swimsuit? What can you add or take away from this swimsuit to make it look better for Toad? Let your creative spirits soar!

Lifesaver Swimming Directions

Frogs love to swim. In fact, they spend most of their time in the water or near the water. When you go swimming, you need to observe certain safety rules that frogs and toads don't need to follow.

Directions: Write your own safety rules on the lifesaver below. Cut it out and glue it onto a piece of cardstock paper or poster board. Hang it up in your classroom or in your room at home to remind yourself of the importance of safety rules when you go swimming.

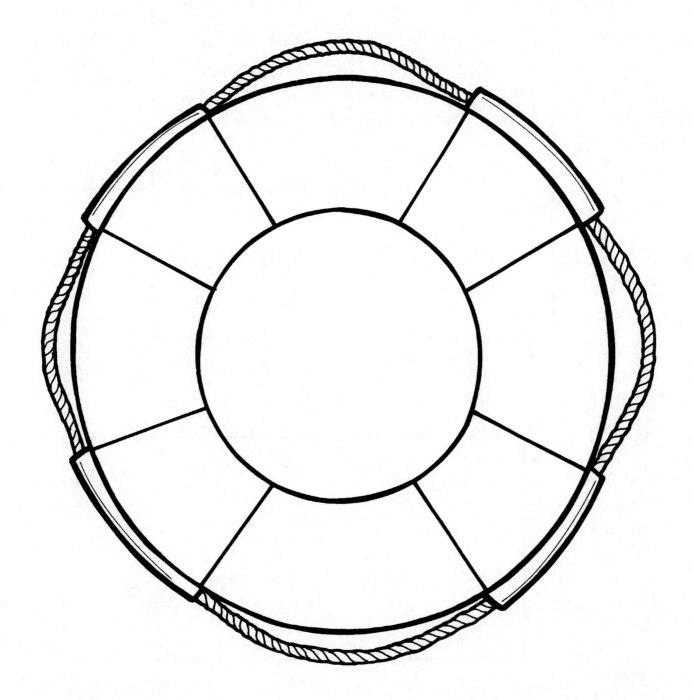

A Letter for Toad

Directions: Toad was lonely and really wanted a letter. Write Toad a friendly letter using the sample below. Don't forget to address the envelope, too.

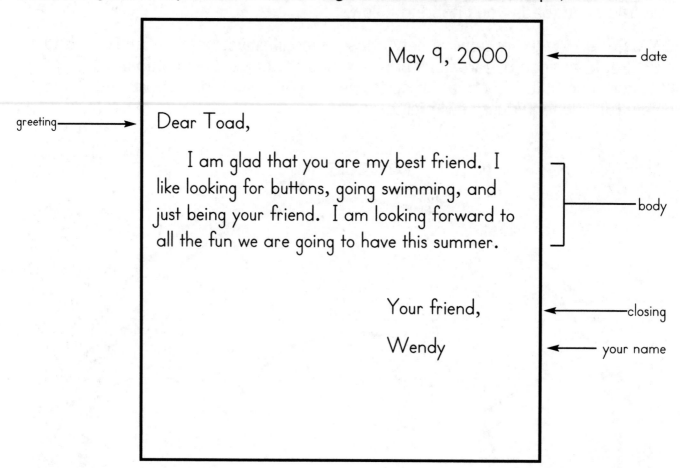

An Envelope for Toad

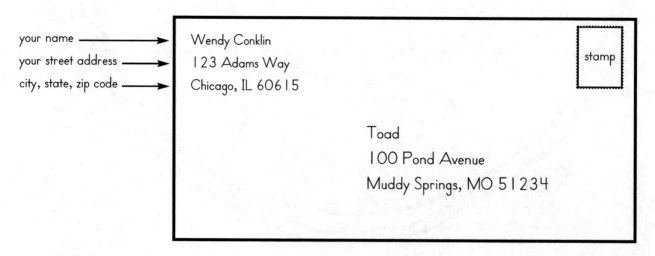

Frog and Toad Stationery

Directions: Use this stationery to write a letter to a friend.

Wanted: A Good Friend

Directions: Frog and Toad are very good friends. How do you know a good friend when you see one? Do you think you are a good friend to someone? Think of words that would describe a friend. Then write a want ad in search of a good friend in the space below.

Frog and Toad Puppet Show

Directions: Students can enjoy a new or old episode of Frog and Toad in the form of a puppet show. Students should team up with a partner for this activity. Have students bring an old, clean sock from home to create their sock puppets in class.

Materials

- old, clean sock from home
- glue
- scissors
- decorative material: fabric scraps, google eyes, buttons, pompoms, yarn, markers, tempera paint, etc.

Directions

1. Using a sock brought from home, each child will create a puppet of either Frog or Toad.

2. Students can use goggle eyes, pompoms, yarn, etc., to enhance their puppets. Let them be creative.

3. After each team of students has a Frog and Toad, have the team practice a dialogue between Frog and Toad. It can be one that is in their book, or it could be created by the students themselves. Use a puppet stage if one is available or make one using sheets of cardboard.

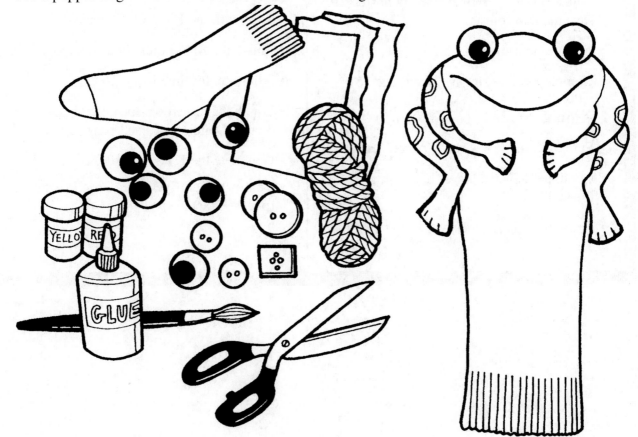

Red Eyed Tree Frog

by Joy Cowley

Summary

Red Eyed Tree Frog *is a book about a frog who lives in the rain forest of Central America. This frog searches for food during the night and also avoids becoming dinner for another animal. The last two pages of the book contain many facts about the red eyed tree frog along with actual-size pictures.*

Below is a three-day plan you could use to adapt to your classroom needs.

Sample Plan

Lesson 1

- Start with the KWL chart (page 25).
- Read *Red Eyed Tree Frog*.
- Begin the Rain Forest in a Box (page 27).
- Discuss Central America and red eyed tree frogs' habitat. Read Protecting the Rain Forest (pages 34–36) and create posters to save the rain forests.
- Allow center time (page 26).
- Complete Measuring by Two (page 55).

Lesson 2

- Start with the KWL chart (page 25).
- Continue the Rain Forest in a Box (page 27).
- Reinforce contractions with What Will the Tree Frog Eat? (pages 28–30).
- Begin making a classroom movie about a night in the life of a tree frog (page 31).
- Label frog body parts (page 33).
- Allow center time (page 26).
- Practice Frog Math (page 57).

Lesson 3

- Start with the KWL chart (page 25).
- Finish the Rain Forest in a Box (page 27).
- Allow center time (page 26).
- Watch the classroom movie and enjoy Toadly Delicious Treats (page 32).
- Complete the KWL chart (page 25).
- Complete Red Eyed Tree Frog Puzzzle (pages 37 and 38).

Overview of Activities

Setting the Stage

1. Prepare your room for a brief study of rain forest frogs by acquiring books on the rain forest.

2. Introduce the KWL chart (page 25) to students. Explain the chart and tell students that it will be on display in the hallway for others to learn with them. Let students complete what they know (K) about tree frogs first. Then, ask if any students have questions (W) about tree frogs.

3. Obtain a large appliance box from a local appliance store for the Rain Forest in a Box activity (page 27). You can paint it in advance if the students are not able to do so. The color green is recommended for the inside and outside.

4. Introduce *Red Eyed Tree Frog*. Show the front cover and have students predict what the book is about. Ask students if they know anything about the red eyed tree frog.

Enjoying the Book

1. Read and discuss *Red Eyed Tree Frog* aloud. Encourage children to predict what will come next on each page. The last two pages of the book give many facts about the red eyed tree frog.

2. Begin with the KWL chart (page 25). Make time each day for students to think about what they have learned (L) about tree frogs. Students can also add questions that they want to know about tree frogs (W).

3. Create a Rain Forest in a Box (page 27). Have students use paper, yarn, felt, stuffed animals, etc., to make the inside of the box look like a rain forest. Students can work on this project as a class, in small groups, or if they finish their required work early.

4. Help students understand where the red eyed tree frog lives by looking at the map on page 36 and locating Central America. Make sure students know that there are many rain forests in the world, but the red eyed tree frog only lives in Central America. Using a globe showing where Central America is in relation to the rest of the world is another option.

5. Divide into groups for Center Time (page 26). This is a flexible activity that can be done each day or all in one day. Divide the room into the Writing Center, Art Center, Reading Center, and Research Center. These four activity centers provide students with the opportunity to learn more about tree frogs and the rain forest.

6. Discuss what would happen to the red eyed tree frog if the rain forest was destroyed in Central America. Students can also donate or raise money to buy a piece of the rain forest. Have students promote awareness by making a poster about saving the rain forest (pages 34–36). Display the posters in the halls at school, in the local libraries, in parents' workplaces, or in grocery stores.

Overview of Activities *(cont.)*

Enjoying the Book (cont.)

---

7. Reinforce contractions with the mini book What Will the Tree Frog Eat? (pages 28–30). Students should fill in the blanks with *will* or *won't*. Then students should color the pictures on each page and cut along the lines. Students should put the pages in correct story order and staple them together to make a mini book.

8. Have students complete the artwork for A Night in the Life of a Tree Frog (page 31). The artwork should be done on construction paper turned vertically. After coloring with dark crayons, students should paint the artwork with black tempera paint and allow to dry overnight. On the next day, connect the drawings top to bottom with clear tape. Attach the first and last drawings to dowels and insert them into a box to make a movie screen. Make Toadly Delicious Treats (page 32) and enjoy the movie.

9. Label a frog's body parts on page 33. Color the frog.

Extending the Book

---

1. Lead students in a measuring activity using yarn with Measuring by Two (page 55). Ask students to compare the red eyed tree frog with regular pond frogs using yarn pieces of 2"–4" (5–10 cm). This activity encourages students to practice multiplication with the number 2 since the pond frogs are twice as big as the red eyed tree frog. Using large chart paper, make a chart of comparative math questions generated from students and put them on display. As students think of other comparison questions, they can add them to the chart. Let students work in pairs or small groups to complete Frog Math (page 57) which contains story problems about the frogs.

2. Have students solve the Red Eyed Tree Frog Puzzle (pages 37 and 38). Students may use information from reference books, books about red eyed tree frogs, the Internet, etc., to find the missing information to solve the puzzle.

3. Remind students to continue making observations about the Tadpole Observation Station (page 63) in their journals.

4. Have students compare pond and rain forest habitats for frogs. Use two large butcher paper sheets to compare similarities and differences about the two environments. Display the chart in the hallway or on a classroom bulletin board.

KWL Chart

A KWL chart is divided into three parts. The first part tells what a child KNOWS (K) about a subject before it is studied in class. The second part tells what the child WANTS (W) to know about that subject. The third part tells what a child LEARNED (L) after studying about that subject.

This should be a class activity facilitated by the teacher.

Directions: Use the drawing below to make 3 large frogs. One frog will have a K, the second frog will have a W, and the last frog will have an L. Provide each child with a set of the KWL frogs to work on at a center or at the student's desk. Have children tape or glue the large KWL frogs onto butcher paper, large sheets of construction paper, or poster board and staple the three sheets. First, have children write what they already know about the rain forest and/or the frogs that live there on the frog with the K. Next, have the children write what they want to know about the rain forest and/or the frogs on the frog with a W. After children have spent time at the learning center and/or completed activities with the class, have them write what they have learned on the frog with an L.

Center Time

Directions: Set up in your room rain forest centers with books, animals, pictures/posters, etc., for children to learn about the frogs that live in the rain forest. Students can rotate through the centers. Suggestions for the centers are listed below. Many of these activities should be introduced to the class with instructions before students work on their own or with partners. Prepare extended activities for enrichment or reinforcement such as the following:

Writing Center

Creative Writing Activity

Students can write an exciting adventure about a trip to the rain forest to find a tree frog. Students can tell what they see, hear, feel, smell, and taste during this adventure. They can also illustrate their stories. To make this center exciting, provide hats, sunglasses, visors, etc., for their adventure into the rain forest. Have a hanging vine (made from yarn) where stories can be attached with clothespins for others to read and enjoy!

Art Center

Frog Rocks

This is a perfect opportunity to allow students to design their own rain forest frog paperweight. The teacher can even have students bring their own rocks to class or let students find them on the playground at school. Have plenty of pictures for students to look at while designing their paperweight. The book *Flashy Fantastic Rain Forest Frogs* by Dorothy Hinshaw Patent is a great resource. There are also wonderful rain forest frog posters that you can purchase from teacher-supply stores. Craft supplies should be abundant to allow for creativity and don't forget to provide smocks for painting.

Research Center

Fact Cards

True and false facts about rain forest frogs can be written on colorful index cards or cardstock. Students can create their own true or false fact cards with the answers on the back to try to stump their classmates. Have students share their cards with others and then grade the results! Display them in the hallway for visitors to answer. If computers are accessible, let students use the Internet for information. Students can also pick a rain forest frog and research it with a partner. Then let students share with the class what they have learned. *Flashy Fantastic Rain Forest Frogs* by Dorothy Hinshaw Patent and *A Walk in the Rainforest* by Kristin Joy Pratt are helpful.

Reading Center

Book Reading Activities

Students write short book reports or summaries about different books that are made available at the reading center. They can also write their own versions of the story in a book. They can also design new covers or bookmarks or write poems about particular books that they read at the reading center.

Rain Forest in a Box

Materials

- appliance box without a top
- green and brown paint
- paintbrushes
- butcher paper in various colors
- green yarn
- chenille sticks
- stuffed animals that represent the types of animals one would find in a rain forest
- construction paper

Directions

1. Paint the outside of the box green and cover it with big green leaves cut from construction paper. As the children learn, these leaves can be used for writing facts about the red eyed tree frog or other frogs that live in the rain forest.

2. After the box has dried, begin creating a rain forest habitat (where the red eyed tree frog lives) inside the box.

3. At the base of the box, cut an oval big enough for a student to crawl through.

4. Large pieces of brown butcher paper can be rolled up lengthwise to be trees with large green construction paper leaves protruding.

5. Yarn can be hung from tree to tree to represent vines.

6. Stuffed animals can be placed inside the box to represent animals found in a rain forest.

7. Each child should then make a tree frog to hang from the trees inside the rain forest box. Don't forget to add a few of the frog's favorite snacks (moths, flies, spiders, grasshoppers). Some predators of the tree frogs should be added as well (bats, snakes).

What Will the Tree Frog Eat?

If we want to say the opposite of "we will," we can say "we will not." Another way to say *will not* is by using the contraction *won't*.

Directions: Fill in the blanks on the following pages with the correct words. Use *will* or the contraction for *will not* to explain what the red eyed tree frog eats. Color the pictures and then cut along the lines. Put each page in correct order according to the *Red Eyed Tree Frog* to make a mini book.

What Will the Tree Frog Eat?

by _____

The red eyed tree frog _____ eat katydids because they are too big to swallow.

What Will the Tree Frog Eat? *(cont.)*

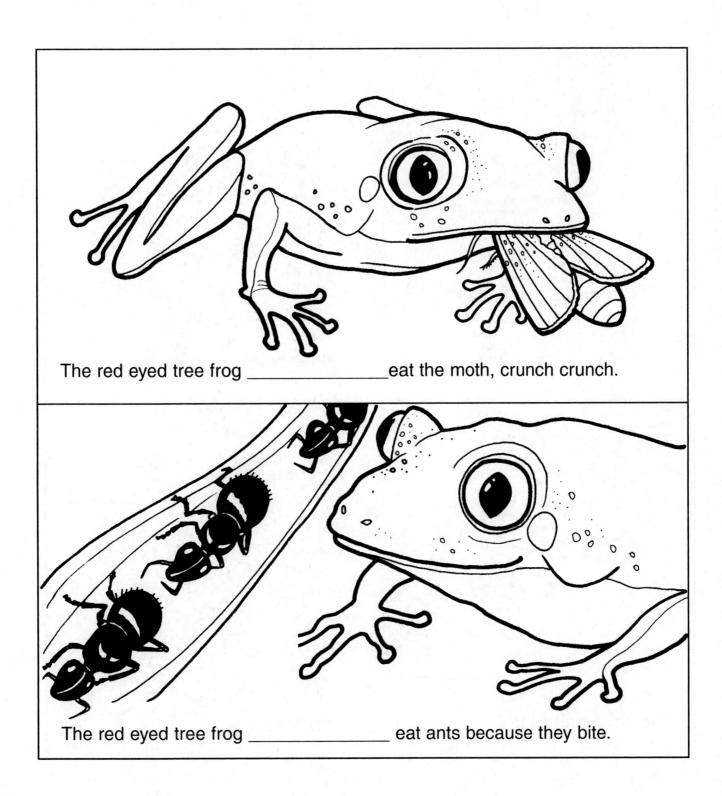

The red eyed tree frog _____eat the moth, crunch crunch.

The red eyed tree frog _____ eat ants because they bite.

What Will the Tree Frog Eat? *(cont.)*

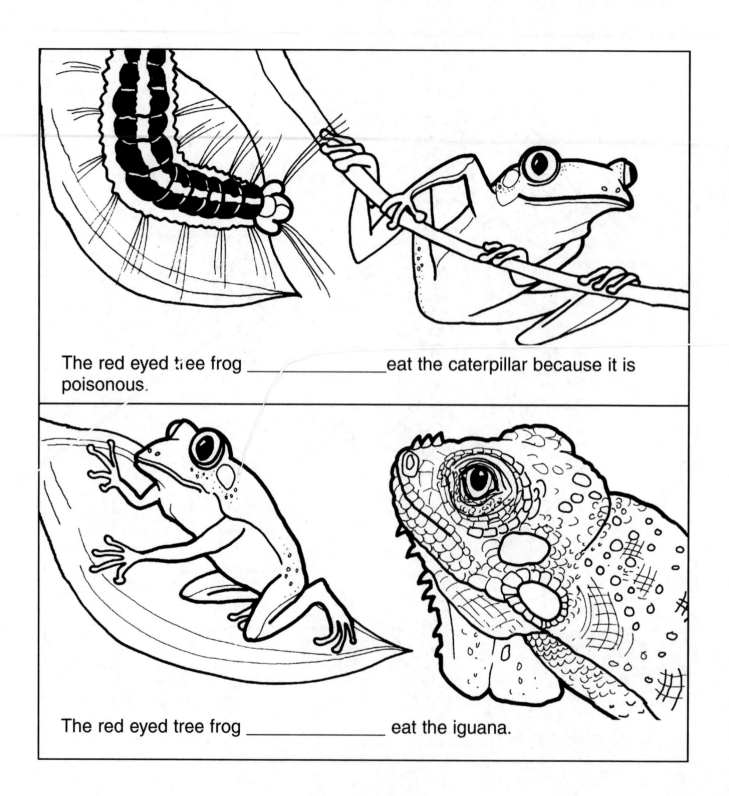

The red eyed tree frog _____ eat the caterpillar because it is poisonous.

The red eyed tree frog _____ eat the iguana.

A Night in the Life of a Tree Frog

Directions: Using crayon-resist art, each student will contribute a drawing to make a classroom movie about a night in the life of a tree frog.

Materials

- white construction paper (per student)
- crayons
- paintbrushes
- cassette
- cassette player

- wooden dowels
- cardboard box
- diluted black tempera paint
- newspaper or butcher paper
- *optional*: musical instruments or rain forest music

Directions

1. Give each child a sheet of white construction paper. Have the children color a scene about a tree frog. Make sure that they color with very dark colors using crayons only. Also the papers should be horizontal so that they are wider.

2. After the children have drawn their pictures, give the students a wide paintbrush and black tempera paint. Have each child lay his or her picture on some butcher paper or newspaper and spread the paint completely over the picture. All of the parts that were not colored will be black (like nighttime), and the other colored parts will show up.

3. After the drawings have completely dried, the teacher should connect the pages side by side and finally connect the first and last pages to the dowels. A large box should be prepared ahead of time to act as a movie screen. Cut holes on the top and bottom sides for the dowels. A large rectangle should be cut in the front of the box so the pictures can be seen as the dowels are rolled.

4. After the movie screen has been assembled, each child will narrate his or her portion on a cassette tape, telling what the tree frog is doing. The teacher could also have rain forest music playing softly in the background, or the students could make the music themselves, using various instruments or sounds to represent animals and nature (rattles, water pouring, bird chirping, insect creaking, etc.).

5. When all of this is completed, have a movie celebration with a rain forest dirt dessert (recipe on page 32). Enjoy the movie!

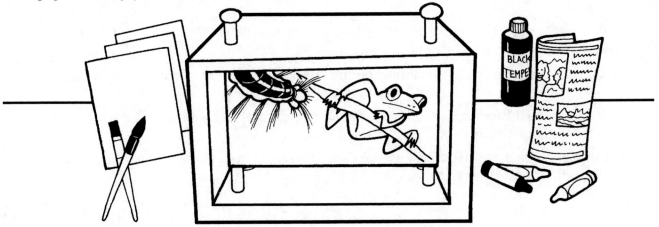

Toadly Delicious Treats

Rain Forest Dirt Dessert

Ingredients

- 1 package (16 oz.) of chocolate cookies, crushed
- 2 cups of cold milk
- 1 package (4-serving size) chocolate instant pudding
- 1 tub (8 oz.) whipped topping, thawed
- 10 small paper or plastic cups
- decorations: gummy worms and frogs, candy flowers, etc.

Directions

1. Crush cookies in a bag with a rolling pin and pour the milk into a large bowl.
2. Add the pudding mix and mix with a wire whisk until blended (1 or 2 minutes). Let the mixture stand for 5 minutes.
3. Stir in whipped topping and half of the crushed cookies.
4. Place 1 tablespoon crushed cookies into cups. Fill cups about ¾ full with pudding mixture. Top each cup with the remaining crushed cookies.
5. Refrigerate the cups for 1 hour. Decorate and enjoy!

Froggy Face Cookies

Ingredients and Materials

- small colorful candy pieces
- black licorice strips cut into approximately 2" (5 cm) sections
- 3 or 4 tubs of white frosting
- green food coloring
- refrigerated sugar cookie dough (Provide enough to make at least one cookie per student.)
- one plastic knife per child
- wax paper

Directions

1. Prior to class, slice and bake the sugar cookies according to the package directions.
2. Give each child one cookie on a piece of wax paper.
3. Mix a few drops of green food coloring into the frosting until it turns a convincing shade of "froggy green."
4. Give each group of four to five children a tub of frosting, a small container filled with small colorful candy pieces, and small pieces of licorice.
5. Let students frost their cookies and use the candy to create "froggy faces." The black licorice works well for the frog's mouth.

Frog Body Parts

Directions: Label the main body parts of a rain forest frog, including the sticky feet, eyes, eardrum, expandable throat, and mouth.

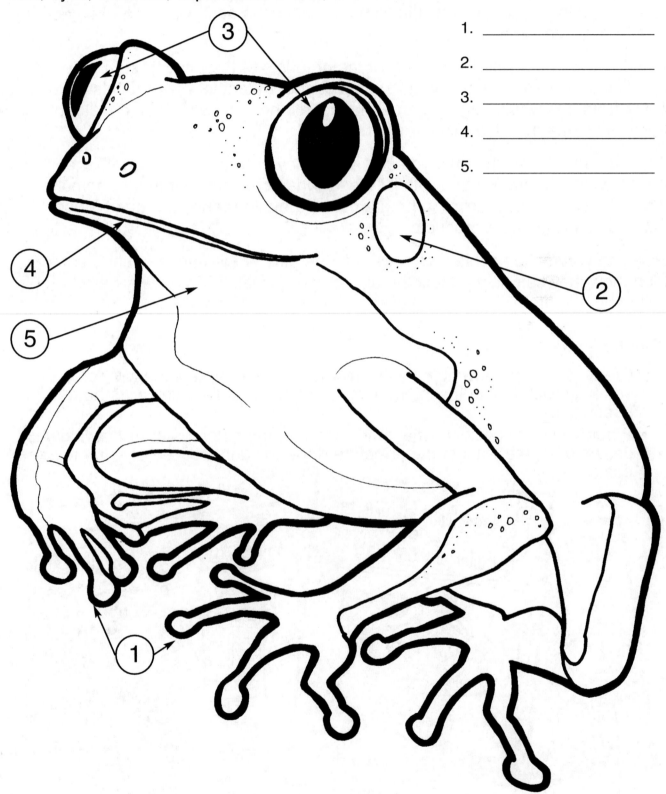

1. _____

2. _____

3. _____

4. _____

5. _____

Protecting the Rain Forest

The rain forest is slowly disappearing because certain companies need land for buildings and because people are using the soil for farming and the trees for their products. If the rain forest in Central America is destroyed, the red eyed tree frog will become extinct.

People around the world use many of the products of the rain forest. Some of the resources can be replaced and some cannot. Many of the products we use come from trees. Although it is true that not all the products used to make paper originally came from the rain forests, many did.

Think about how much paper you use in one day. What do you do with the paper when you are finished with it? Today, many people, whether at home, work, or school, have recycling programs that help to reduce our need for so much paper and paper products.

How can you make people more aware of the gifts of the rain forest and show them how they can help protect the plants and animals? Some ways are to write about it, draw pictures, or tell people what they need to know.

Activity

- Create a poster showing people why they need to protect the rain forests. You may wish to use the information on page 35 to help you with the rain forest facts.
- When you have decided what to include on the poster, practice drawing your design on some butcher paper before drawing your finalized design on your poster.

Protecting the Rain Forest *(cont.)*

Rain Forest Facts

Although most of us live far from the world's rain forests, they touch our lives in some way every day. If you have ever eaten a chocolate bar, sipped a cup of tea, or eaten a banana, you have used a product that came from some part of a rain forest. In the United States, we grow many citrus fruits, but did you know that oranges, grapefruits, and pineapples are all plants that originated in the rain forests?

Here are some other facts about products that come from the rain forest. Use the following information and other facts you find in books to help you with the poster project on page 34.

Cocao Trees

These trees grow wild in the Amazon rain forest. They provide us with the beans that we use to make chocolate. Although today most cocoa comes from large tree farms, the trees on the farms all originated in the rain forest.

Manioc

Manioc is a root that provides many people in tropical rain forests with the starch they need for food. You may have eaten a product of the manioc root for dessert. What is it? Tapioca!

Rubber

Rubber is another product now grown on tree farms, but these trees originally came from the rain forest. The tree's inner bark contains a liquid called latex. When the latex is heated or mixed with chemicals, tiny bits in the liquid stick together and form a solid lump of rubber. Think about how many products around you that are made from rubber or have rubber as part of their product.

Protecting the Rain Forest *(cont.)*

Rain Forest Facts *(cont.)*

Kapok Tree

The kapok tree belongs to a large group of trees that grow to be 130 feet (40 meters) or more in height. Its short, elastic fibers are used in making upholstery and floss. The seed oil of the kapok tree is used in the manufacture of soap. The fiber, or kapok, is water repellent. (Water will not soak into it.) Large amounts of kapok are used to produce life preservers and other water repellent products.

Where Are the Rain Forests?

This map shows where on Earth the rain forests are located. The areas in black are the rain forests. As you can see, not much of the earth's land has rain forests! It is important that we protect them.

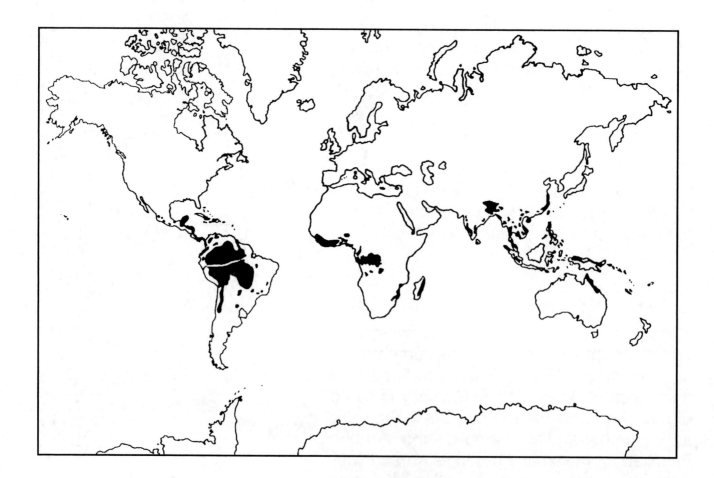

Red Eyed Tree Frog Puzzle

Directions: Use research information from books, encyclopedias, and the Internet to complete the puzzle on page 38.

Down

1. The red eyed tree frog belongs to the genus _____ .

2. The red eyed tree frog is an animal that stays awake at night or is _____ .

3. This frog species is primarily found in _____ America.

4. These frogs are not herbivores because they are meat eaters or _____ .

5. Red eyed tree frogs reproduce by laying _____ .

Across

6. Red eyed tree frogs have _____-cup toes.

7. These frogs inhabit tropical _____ areas.

8. _____ is a threat to the frogs' habitat.

9. This frog belongs to the _____ family classification.

10. While it sleeps during the day, a red eyed tree frog could use its _____ for defense.

Red Eyed Tree Frog

Red Eyed Tree Frog Puzzle *(cont.)*

Tuesday

by David Wiesner

Summary

One Tuesday evening around 8:00 P.M., frogs begin to fly atop their magical lily pads and explore the local neighborhood. Every few pages tells a different time until dawn begins to break and the spell is broken. The neighborhood is left with clues of the night before as the police and investigators try to piece together the happenings. The following Tuesday begins another mysterious adventure that only one's imagination could tell.

Below is a sample lesson plan that could adapt to a particular classroom's needs.

Sample Plan

Lesson 1

- Read *Tuesday* to the class while showing the book.
- Begin working on the *Tuesday* story mobile (page 42).
- Play the bulletin board game (pages 72 and 73).
- Report the news surrounding the events in *Tuesday* (page 44).
- Continue making journal entries about the Tadpole Observation Station (page 63).
- Create a new dictionary (page 51).
- Create one of the Frog and Toad Art Projects (pages 67–69).

Lesson 2

- Create a mini-animation frog book (page 43).
- Play the bulletin board game (pages 72 and 73).
- Complete *Tuesday* story mobile (page 42).
- Make paper jumping frogs (page 45).
- Complete the activity Graphing a Frog Jump (page 46).
- Begin work on the weekday book (page 43).
- Practice spelling games (page 53).
- Create one of the Frog and Toad Art Projects (pages 67–69).

Lesson 3

- Write a friendship recipe (page 50).
- Complete work on weekday books and share them with the class (page 43).
- Practice time chronology with Arriving on Time (page 47).
- Design a Pond (page 60).
- Practice spelling games (page 53).
- Continue making journal entries about the Tadpole Observation Station (page 63).
- Play the bulletin board game (pages 72 and 73).
- Practice direction skills with An Evening Stroll in the Neighborhood (page 48).
- Do the Frog Word Search (page 54).
- Begin fingerpainting for the culminating activity (page 70).

Lesson 4

- Begin creating a Classroom Frog Life Cycle Book (page 70).
- Compare rain forest frogs and pond frogs on a Venn diagram (page 64).

Lesson 5

- Complete creating a Classroom Frog Life Cycle Book (page 70).

Overview of Activities

Setting the Stage

1. Show the cover of the book and ask for ideas on what this book might be about.

2. Explain the difference between fiction and nonfiction. Compare the two previous books. Based on its cover, can students tell if *Tuesday* is fiction or nonfiction?

3. Prepare the bulletin board games (pages 72 and 73). Lily pads cut from paper can be used as the spaces the students will hop to.

Enjoying the Book

1. Read Tuesday to the class. Then allow students to reread the book, looking at the details on each page.

2. Create Tuesday story mobiles (page 42). Let students be as creative as they want. Hang some of the mobiles around the classroom.

3. Write paragraphs for Here's the News! (page 44). This a perfect opportunity for students to learn how to write an informative paragraph which should include the 5 W's: what, where, when, who, why, (and how). Guide students through the process using another book that the class knows well. Then have students write a paragraph for Tuesday. This can also be done as a class activity on a chart at the front of the room for those who do not write well.

4. Let students create and draw their own mini-animation frog books (page 43). Let students exchange their books with one another after each student has created his or her own frog book.

5. Make paper jumping frogs (page 45) with the students. Let students decorate their frogs. Then hold a jumping contest with the Graphing a Frog Jump activity (page 46). The paper frog jumping contest should be done one frog at a time. Make a large cardboard playing mat with a starting line. Each student should jump his or her frog by pressing down on the tail and then releasing it. The length of the frog jump should be marked with a pencil and the student's name. Have students record the length jumped on a bulletin board bar graph, using centimeters as the measurement. You can also have students record the top five measurements of their classmates on a bar graph on their own paper. As an added activity, hold a jumping contest for the students themselves.

6. For the Weekday Book activity (page 43), divide students into groups of four or five. Lead a brainstorming activity and allow the groups to discuss what kind of book they could write about but remind students to select a day of the week other than Tuesday and to use certain creatures other than frogs. Give the groups three days to complete the book including a short text and illustrations in their groups.

7. Students practice telling time with the activity Arriving on Time (page 47). This activity allows students to cut out and glue the different times in chronological order. As an extension to this activity, teachers may want to ask students to write their daily schedules from the time they wake up to the time they go to sleep.

Overview of Activities *(cont.)*

Enjoying the Book (cont.)

8. Understanding directions is the concept involved in An Evening Stroll in the Neighborhood (page 48). Students trace the path the frogs flew in Tuesday. As an extension to this activity, teachers may want to ask students to write directions from their homes to school or vice versa.

9. Complete Frog Word Search (page 54).

Extending the Book

1. Play the bulletin board game (pages 72 and 73). This game is easily adapted to any subject, but it is focused on learning to tell time. Each student will need one frog playing piece (page 73). One die and one clock will be needed for this activity as well.

2. Create a new dictionary on page 51 using illustrated pictures. Have students write the word on the page but draw a picture to explain what the word means. Staple the pages together to make a book.

3. Practice spelling with the spelling games on page 53. A word list is provided on page 52.

4. Write a recipe for friendship on page 50. Bring in recipe books for students to look at and get ideas from. Students should be encouraged to be creative.

5. After brainstorming about what frogs need in order to live, have students design their own pond environment for a frog (page 60). Students can do this individually on construction paper or as a class project on large sheets of butcher paper.

6. Don't forget to record observations in the Tadpole Observation Station journals (page 63).

7. Now that students have learned about some different types of frogs, teachers may want to ask students to create a Venn diagram to compare rain forest frogs and pond frogs (page 64).

8. Encourge students to make some of the Frog and Toad Art Projects described on pages 67–69. These may be displayed during open house or taken home as decorative gifts for friends and family.

9. As a culminating activity for this unit, students will create a Classroom Frog Life Cycle Book (page 70) using an Eric Carle book as a model to follow. Students will fingerpaint large sheets of glossy paper. Students will work in groups, and each group will create a fingerpainted representation of a stage of the frog life cycle. After each group has completed their stage of the life cycle, the class will create a story for their classroom book.

Tuesday Story Mobile

Look at the pictures in the book *Tuesday* once again. Choose five or six pictures and think about what might be happening in each. Follow the directions below to make a mobile that describes each picture you choose.

Materials

- construction paper or unlined index cards
- yarn
- hole punch
- paper towel cardboard tube
- scissors
- glue or tape
- crayons and markers

Directions

1. Draw pictures from the story on the construction paper or unlined index cards. Color your pictures.

2. Cut out the pictures.

3. On the back of each picture, write a short story about it.

4. Punch a hole at the top of each picture and tie a piece of yarn to each one. (The yarn should be different lengths.)

5. Make four slits in the cardboard tube as shown in the illustration.

6. Force the yarn through the slit and secure it with a knot.

7. Hang your mobile by another length of yarn tied at the center of the tube. (You may need to tape the center yarn to prevent it from sliding once you have the mobile balanced.)

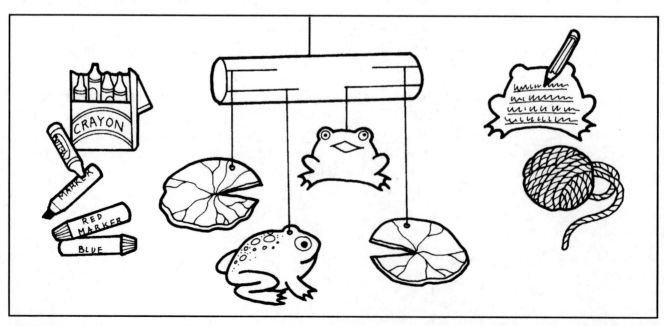

42

Creative Projects

Here are some creative projects that students can work on individually or in groups.

Weekday Book

Group students together in groups of four or five to create their own weekday books. They are to choose a day of the week to name the book (any but Tuesday) and choose a creature that will fly through the air investigating the sights on the way. Have each student use large construction paper (11" x 16" or 25 cm x 41 cm size) to illustrate what happens in his or her story step by step. The group must work together. Each student should complete at least one page. On each page have the students tell the time that this event is occurring. Bind the pages together and have each group share their story with the rest of the class.

Mini-Animation Frog Book

Staple (along either the left or right side) 6–8 blank index cards (any size can be used but 3" x 5" or 8 cm x 13 cm is suggested). Draw pictures of frogs in different positions or moving in various ways. Color your pictures and show your mini-animation book to your friend or classmate.

Here's the News!

Directions: As a reporter for the local evening news, you have been given the assignment of reporting about the events of *Tuesday*. Write a paragraph to tell what happened on the day that the frogs began to fly. Answer the questions below to write your paragraph.

NEWS

What happened? _____

_____

Where did it happen? _____

_____

When did it happen? _____

_____

Who did it happen to? _____

_____

Why did it happen? _____

_____

How did it happen? _____

_____

Paper Jumping Frogs

Directions: Have you ever been to a frog jumping contest? Follow the directions below to make a paper jumping frog. These frogs will compete at a frog jumping contest. The results of the contest will be displayed on a bar graph. You will need a 3½" x 5" index card or tagboard.

1. Fold top right corner over to the left edge. Unfold it.
2. Fold top left corner over to the right edge. Unfold it.
3. Fold the top ⅓ of the card down. Unfold it.
4. Push in the sides of the card at points 1 and 2. Then fold down.
5. Lift points 3 and 4 and fold up.
6. Fold in points 5 and 6.
7. Fold bottom half of card up.
8. Fold half of that under.
9. Decorate your frog.

To make your frog jump, push on the back of its tail and release it quickly. The quicker you push and release, the further it will go.

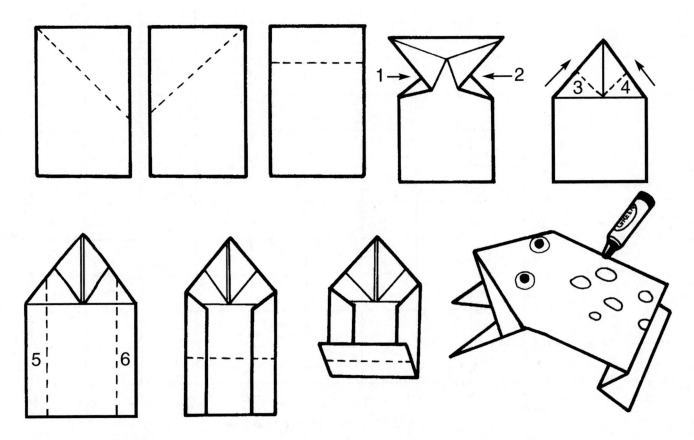

Graphing a Frog Jump

Directions: On the bar graph below, color in the correct number of squares to represent how many centimeters your frog jumped. Record your classmates' results, too.

Name of Frog   **Paper Frog Jump Results**

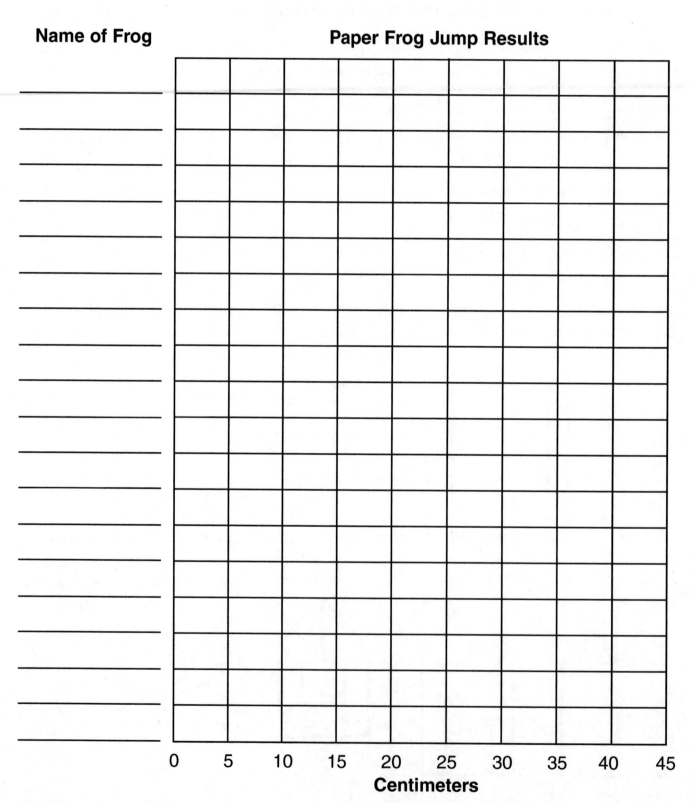

0   5   10   15   20   25   30   35   40   45

Centimeters

Arriving on Time

As the frogs flew through the neighborhood during the night on Tuesday, the time changed from P.M. to A.M. at 12:00 midnight. The P.M. hours begin at noon and end at midnight. The A.M. hours begin at midnight and end at noon. For example, 12:00 P.M. is at lunchtime, and 12:00 A.M. is during the nighttime.

Directions: Below are 10 houses with clocks from that neighborhood. Cut and paste these houses in the correct order. Start with 8:00 P.M. and end with 8:00 A.M.

12:00 A.M.	8:00 P.M.	7:00 A.M.	1:00 A.M.	9:00 P.M.
3:00 A.M.	5:00 A.M.	11:00 P.M.	8:00 A.M.	4:00 A.M.

An Evening Stroll in the Neighborhood

Follow these directions through the neighborhood and trace the path the frogs flew in *Tuesday*.

1. Beginning at the pond, go straight down Spring Street.
2. Turn left on Tree Frog Avenue.
3. Turn right on Lily Pond Road.
4. Turn right on Green Drive.
5. Turn left on Spring Street.
6. Turn right on Pollywog Road.
7. Turn right on Insect Boulevard.
8. Turn right on Tree Frog Avenue.
9. Turn right on Leaping Lane.
10. Turn left on Green Drive.
11. Turn left on Spring Street and follow it back to the pond.

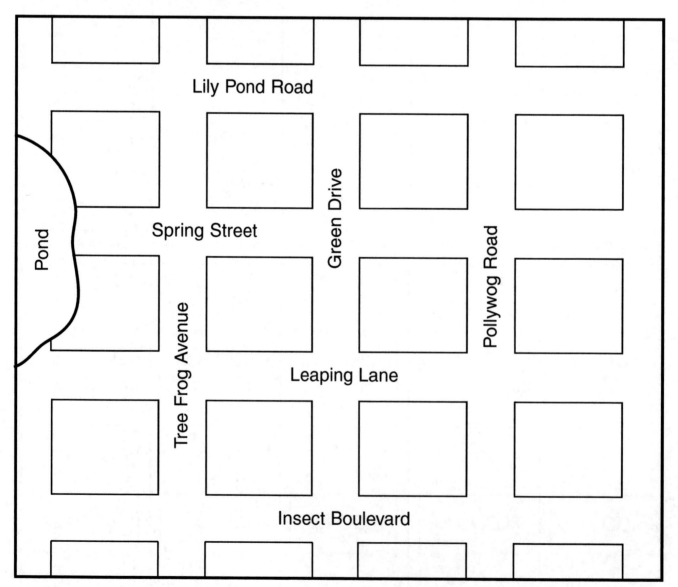

Frog and Toad Poetry

Teacher Note: *Poetry is a wonderful way to entice children into creatively expressing their ideas about the information they are learning. Have students brainstorm words or phrases about frogs and toads from what they have learned in this unit. Display the list in a prominent place. Copy the information below and distribute copies to the students. Model the poems below to show students how to create their own frog and toad poetry. Ask students to illustrate their completed poems.*

Diamante

A *diamante* is a diamond-shaped poem about opposites. To write a diamante about a frog, think about opposites. For example, how different is the frog at the beginning stages of its life (tadpole, for example) from the way it looks when it becomes a frog? Create the diamond-shaped poem (diamante), using the following pattern:

- Lines 1 and 7 state the opposites.
- Lines 2 and 6 state two adjectives that describe the opposite closest to it.
- Lines 3 and 5 state "ing" words that describe the opposite closest to it.
- Line 4 contains four nouns. The first two nouns describe the first opposite, and the second opposite is described by the last two nouns.

Tadpole
Tiny, Green
Wriggling, Swimming, Eating
Gills, Tail, Lungs, Legs
Hopping, Croaking, Hiding
Bulbous, Eye-popping,
Frog

Recipe for a Perfect Friendship

Toad baked some cookies for his friend Frog. Think about what it takes to have a friendship. Make up a recipe for a perfect friendship. Write it on the lines below.

— A Perfect Friendship —

Ingredients

_____

_____

_____

_____

_____

Directions

_____

_____

_____

_____

_____

_____

_____

Bake at _____ degrees for _____ minutes.

Share it with a friend.

A New Dictionary

Directions: Not all dictionaries have words to describe meanings. Some pictionary dictionaries use pictures to explain meanings. Make a picture card dictionary for all the terms that have to do with the frog unit. Using a 5" x 8" (13 cm x 20 cm) card for each word, write the word at the bottom of the unlined side of the card and illustrate the word. On the back of the lined side of the card, write a definition of what the word means. Here are some words you could choose from: *amphibian, bullfrog, croak, frog, frog legs, froglet, gills, green, hibernate, insects, jump, leap, life cycle, lily pad, lungs, metamorphosis, pollywogs, pond, splash, tadpole, toad, tree frog, warts, water.*

Sample

Frog

an aquatic amphibian with smooth, moist skin
and webbed feet; has long hind legs that are
used for jumping

Spelling Word List

Directions: Here are some spelling words that can be used to play some of the spelling games on page 53.

frog	smooth	rain forest	gills
toad	tree frog	leaves	pollywog
pond	tadpole	moist	lungs
water	insects	legs	metamorphosis
bumpy	suckers	leap	amphibian
jump	green	spring	hibernate
eggs	cycle	croak	tail

Spelling Games

Frog Baseball

Students hop from base to base as they spell words correctly.

Preparation

The game should be set up like a baseball field in the classroom. There should be three bases (white construction paper squares) and a home plate where the "batter" will stand to spell the word. The pitcher's mound can be where an opposing team member or the teacher can call out the words to be spelled.

Game Directions and Rules

The student at bat must spell the word correctly to advance to first base. As other students spell words correctly, they continue to advance the bases to home plate. When a player reaches home plate, a point is scored for the team. If a student misses a word, it is counted as one out. When a batting team has three outs, they switch with the opposing team who then has a turn at bat. Each team should be given equal turns to bat, much like innings. Decide on how many innings will be played before the game begins. The team with the most points at the end wins. Words can also be categorized as singles (easy words), doubles (slightly difficult), triples (more difficult), and home runs (very difficult). Be aware that sometimes this can cause pressure on weaker spellers who could successfully spell a word that would be a single but might choose a harder word and cause their team an out.

Around the Pond

Students advance from lily pad to lily pad as they compete with a classmate in spelling.

Preparation

Find an open space large enough to play the game. There should be one less lily pad than there are students in the class. Everyone has a lily pad (pieces of construction paper) except one student who shares a lily pad with another student.

Game Directions and Rules

The two students who share a lily pad compete to spell a word. The teacher reads a word and the first person to say the word has the opportunity to spell the word. That student is given 10 seconds to spell the word. Only one chance is allowed. If the student spells the word correctly, that student advances to the next lily pad and competes again with another student and a new word. If the student does not spell the word correctly, the other student is allowed a turn to spell the word. If both students miss the word, the students on the next two lily pads become competing partners sharing a lily pad. The game is played until the teacher decides the time is up.

Frog Word Search

Directions: Find all the words listed below in the word search. Words may be down, across, backwards, or diagonal.

jump	smooth	tadpole	green
bumpy	tree	pond	insects
eggs	toad	water	
frog	suckers		

```
a  o  u  k  t  j  s  h  p  m  u  j  a  z  k
d  a  u  i  a  q  d  n  h  q  l  b  l  g  l
s  v  b  f  g  f  m  w  r  s  s  o  t  s  b
w  p  i  c  r  b  s  j  m  u  l  m  a  t  u
p  c  d  e  n  o  g  o  c  a  f  o  d  m  p
i  a  t  u  v  o  g  k  o  p  d  g  p  p  o
b  a  o  k  e  h  e  w  a  d  k  q  o  k  n
w  h  s  g  v  r  b  l  i  a  o  n  l  i  d
c  w  t  w  s  c  l  k  x  o  g  i  e  e  q
f  z  c  d  i  v  a  e  l  t  m  w  z  w  c
t  y  e  w  b  v  j  r  c  a  g  h  q  u  f
r  g  s  h  s  m  o  o  t  h  o  r  z  l  w
e  m  n  a  u  c  g  u  l  d  o  v  e  m  g
e  q  i  d  n  h  c  a  m  y  s  x  n  e  d
z  x  u  b  y  p  m  u  b  t  n  h  l  m  n
```

Measuring by Two

Directions: Measure the difference between red eyed tree frogs and regular pond frogs. Using yarn, cut a 2-inch (5-cm) piece to represent the red eyed tree frog and then cut a 4-inch (10-cm) piece to represent a pond frog.

1. What do you see when you compare the lengths of these two frogs?

   _____

2. How many tree frogs would it take to equal the length of one regular frog?

   _____

Try to solve the questions below by multiplying the tree frog results by 2. Do you see a pattern?

3. How many tree frogs would it take, when lined up front to back, to measure your desk?_____

4. How many pond frogs would measure the length of your desk?_____

5. How many tree frogs tall are you?_____

6. How many pond frogs tall are you? _____

7. How many tree frogs tall is your teacher? _____

8. How many pond frogs tall is your teacher? _____

Extension: Can you think of any other questions to add to the list? Write them on the back of this page.

Frog Facts

Directions: After solving the problems at the bottom of the page, fill in the missing letters to answer each question.

1. This amphibian lives in the rain forest of Central America.

__ __ __   __ __ __ __   __ __ __ __   __ __ __ __
13 4 3   4 16 4 3   15 13 4 4   5 13 11 6

2. A tadpole breathes with __ __ __ __ __.
                            6 7 9 9 14

3. Another name for pollywog is __ __ __ __ __ __ __.
                                15 1 3 12 11 9 4

4. A frog can breathe through its __ __ __ __.
                                  14 8 7 10

5. Frogs mainly eat __ __ __ __ __ __ __.
                    7 10 14 4 2 15 14

8 + 8 = Y	1 − 0 = A	7 − 5 = C	5 + 4 = L
8 + 6 = S	8 − 5 = D	2 + 2 = E	15 − 3 = P
15 − 5 = N	10 + 1 = O	12 − 5 = I	8 + 7 = T
10 − 5 = F	5 + 3 = K	4 + 2 = G	5 + 8 = R

Frog Math

Directions: Answer each question below about tadpoles and frogs.

1. 34 eggs in the pond

   + 15 more eggs were laid
   _____

   How many in all? _____

2. 78 eggs under a leaf

   − 53 eggs hatched
   _____

   How many eggs were left? _____

3. 41 tadpoles swam downstream

   + 26 tadpoles joined them
   _____

   How many tadpoles altogether?
   _____

4. 99 tadpoles swam in the pond

   − 62 frogs swam in the pond
   _____

   How many more tadpoles than
   frogs swam in the pond? _____

5. 87 tree frogs on a tree

   − 11 snakes eat a tree frog each
   _____

   How many tree frogs are left? _____

6. 64 toads were croaking in the pond

   + 24 toads joined the fun
   _____

   How many toads were in the pond?

   _____

7. 78 toads ate flies

   + 16 toads also ate flies
   _____

   How many toads ate flies? _____

8. 55 toads were sitting on lily pads

   − 15 left the lily pads
   _____

   How many toads were left
   sitting on the lily pads? _____

9. 44 frogs were sleeping

   + 15 toads were also sleeping
   _____

   How many frogs and toads
   were sleeping? _____

10. 61 tadpoles were eating

    − 17 tadpoles were not eating
    _____

    How many tadpoles were eating? _____

Frog Leg Measuring

Directions: Cut out the frog leg on the following page to help you measure the distances in your classroom. This frog leg equals one foot or 12 inches (30 cm).

1. How many frog legs is it from the math table to the computer? _____

2. How many frog legs is it around the teacher's desk? _____

3. How long (measured in frog legs) is the blackboard? _____

4. How many frog legs is it from your desk to a friend's desk? _____

5. How many frog legs is it from the north wall to the south wall in your classroom? _____

6. How tall (measured in frog legs) is a friend? _____

7. How many frog legs is it to the principal's office? _____

8. How many frog legs is it to the nearest drinking fountain? _____

Frog Leg Measuring *(cont.)*

Directions: Cut out the patterns and attach the top of the leg to the bottom by gluing tab A where indicated below.

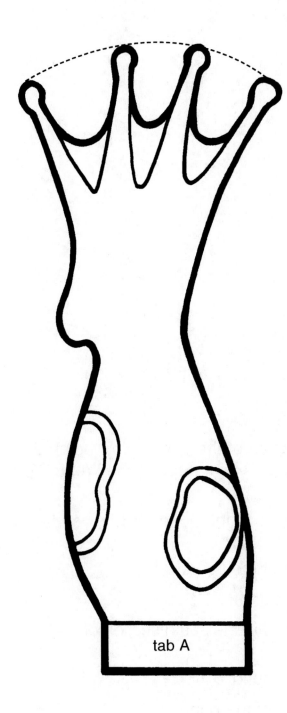

tab A

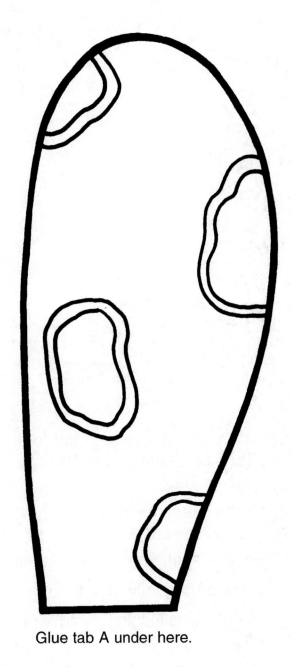

Glue tab A under here.

Design a Pond

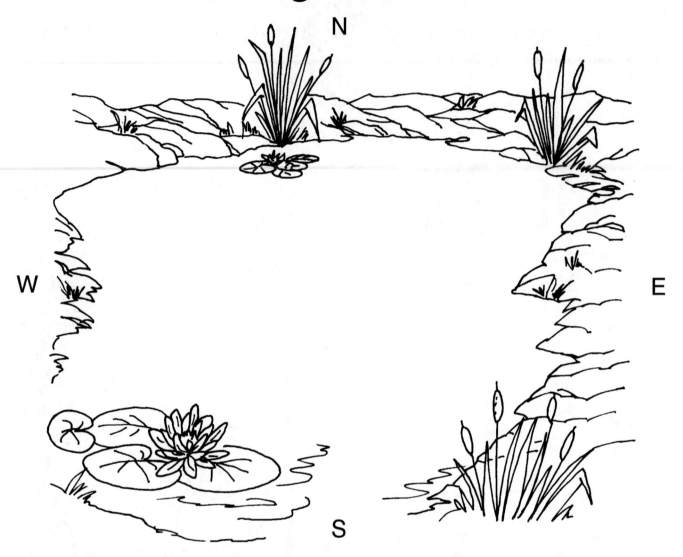

Look at the pond above. Point to the **North** section of the pond. Now point to the **East** side of the pond. Point to the **South** side. Now point to the **West**. You are ready to begin.

Follow the directions below to show all the animals in the pond. When you finish you may color your pond map.

1. Draw a snapping turtle in the south section of the pond.

2. Draw a dragonfly over the north part of the pond.

3. Show a frog leaping off a lily pad into the pond in the south section of the pond.

4. Draw a school of fish in the west part of the pond.

5. Show a duck swimming in the south section of the pond.

6. Draw a bat flying over the east part of the pond.

Seasons of the Pond

The Pond in Spring

As winter ends the days gradually warm and grow longer. With the increase in daylight hours, pond plants begin their race for a place in the sun. Spring has arrived at the pond. The duckweeds and algae are among the first plants to show their growth because they're small and need little food. All around the pond and in the marshy areas along the river, irises, reeds, and other plants are beginning to unfold their green shoots and leaves. As the sun's warmth spreads through the water, animals in the weeds and in the mud at the bottom of the pond awaken. Frogs, toads, fish, and newts court, mate, and lay eggs. Their eggs soon hatch in the warmer water, and the energetic offspring set off in search of their next meal. The cold-blooded animals become more active as the water temperature rises, and with this increase in activity comes an increase in hunger. The pond is teeming with life in the spring. Finding food is much easier now than in the long, cold winter.

The Pond in Summer

Summer is a time for pond plants to grow and become thick and lush. The amount of growth and kinds of plants depends mainly on how much sunlight the pond receives. Only a large growth of plant life will provide the food, shelter, and places for nesting required by the pond animals.

In early summer, pond animals feed heartily and fatten up. Tadpoles, insect larvae, and other small creatures hungrily feed on the rich plant growth. These animals are also known as herbivores because they eat only plants. Larger animals such as newts and small fish feed on these smaller herbivores and also pond animals such as frogs, fish, and snails. These animals are called carnivores because they eat only meat. In this way the pond food chain is created.

All plants and animals in the pond will eventually die, and this too helps the living creatures in the pond. Animal remains and droppings enrich the water by providing food for some animals and minerals for fresh plant growth. Nothing is wasted; everything is recycled in the pond.

The Pond in Autumn

As summer ends and the days grow shorter, the pond animals slow down and prepare for winter. Some of the smaller water creatures are busy laying eggs now, for these animals will die before the winter comes. Their eggs will hatch in the spring, bringing new life. Some types of ducks and geese fly south in anticipation of the cold weather, while the animals that stay stuff themselves on ripe fruit. They are building up fat stores for the long winter that lies ahead.

Many of the pond plants that were green and lush in the spring and summer are drying out and dying in the fall. But even as they die, insects, animals, and the wind are scattering the seeds that will burst forth with new life in the spring.

The Pond in Winter

During the long, cold days of winter, fish, water mollusks, and worms move to the deepest part of the pond where they won't be iced in. Their bodies cool off and slow down so they can survive with much less food and oxygen. Other small pond creatures lay eggs in the autumn before they die. The eggs lie dormant through the winter, and they hatch in spring. Frogs and toads find a protected place on land and hibernate until spring. Winter is a quiet, sleepy time at the pond.

Seasons of the Pond *(cont.)*

Comprehension Questions

Answer the following questions after reading the information on page 61.

1. What happens to the daylight hours and temperatures in spring?

   _____

   _____

2. How do pond animals and plants respond to spring time changes?

   _____

   _____

3. What is a pond food chain? Describe.

   _____

   _____

4. How do the remains of plants and animals help the pond environment?

   _____

   _____

5. What happens to pond plants and animals in the autumn? Describe.

   _____

   _____

6. Why is it easier for pond animals to find food in the spring than it is in the winter?

   _____

   _____

7. What do you do in the spring that is different from what you do in the winter?

   _____

   _____

8. How are you like a pond animal in the winter? How are you different?

   _____

   _____

62

Tadpole Observation Station

Before you begin your frog unit, have tadpoles shipped in time for the opening day. One place to order from is listed below.

Insect Lore
P.O. Box 1535
132 S. Beech St.
Shafter, CA 93263
1-800-LIVE BUG
www.insectlore.com

An aquarium or small fish container should be on display so that students can make observations in a journal. You can have students make journal entries daily or every 3 days. Students can use small spiral notebooks or a personalized homemade notebook with copies of the following pages below stapled together. In their journal they should draw what they see and write a few sentences about what they see. Since the process can take 2–3 months, many teachers prefer to have students write in their journal at least twice a week. To make this learning center irresistible, have it stocked with resource books about frogs as well as an audio tape of frog sounds. Helpful tips: Make sure you use spring water or pond water and replace the water twice a week. Algae fish food is a good source of food for the tadpoles and can be purchased at a pet store. Another idea is to get your own tadpoles from a local creek or pond. This can be done in the spring around the month of March. (Bullfrog tadpoles work great and can be used to compare with other regular tadpoles.)

Life Cycle Journal

Make a journal from the pages below. Make 3 copies (per student) and cut them along the dashed lines. Staple them together at the end.

Date _____

Today I observed_____

_____

_____

_____

_____

_____

_____

Date _____

Today I observed_____

_____

_____

_____

_____

_____

_____

Frog and Toad Venn Diagram

After reading *Discovering What Frogs and Toads Do* by Seymour Simon, decide which words describe a frog and which describe a toad. Venn diagrams help us organize what we know. Correctly place the descriptions inside the frog or toad shape. If some descriptions apply to both, write them on the lily pad that is shared.

- hopping
- leaping
- webbed toes
- green
- brown

- smooth
- moist
- short legs
- long legs
- thinner

- teeth
- long jumps
- dry
- bumpy
- plump

- eats live insects
- lives near water
- lives away from water
- lays eggs in water

Extension

A large Venn diagram can be made by hanging two hula hoops on the bulletin board with paper behind it. Students can write the information in the circles.

Have students compare land frogs and water frogs.

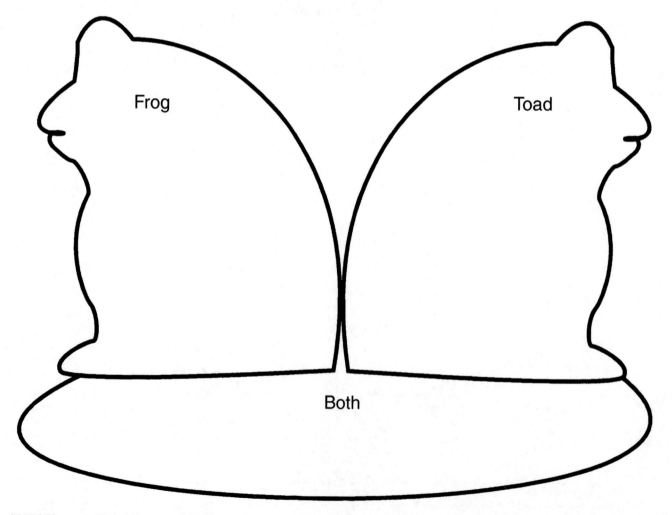

The Life Cycle of an Amphibian

Read the following information about amphibians. Use what you learned about the life cycle of the amphibian to complete the activity on page 66.

Frogs, toads, newts, and salamanders all belong to a group of animals called amphibians. An amphibian lays its eggs, called spawn, in water. The spawn are covered in a kind of jelly to protect them from other animals and bacteria. The tiny eggs soon hatch into very small animals called tadpoles. These tadpoles breathe through gills and don't look or act like their parents at all.

At first, the tiny tadpoles eat plants, but soon they begin to feed on small water animals. They also begin to grow front legs. Soon their back legs begin to grow, and their tails become shorter and eventually disappear.

By this time, the tiny animal has developed lungs and no longer breathes through gills. The amphibian is now a small version of its adult parent. The salamander, newt, and toad will leave the ponds and rivers for a while, but the frog stays close to the water all its life.

All amphibians will one day come back to the water to lay eggs and begin the cycle again.

The Life Cycle of an Amphibian *(cont.)*

Activity

Cut out the boxes at the bottom of the page. Glue them to the following amphibian life cycle chart to show the correct order of the stages of development.

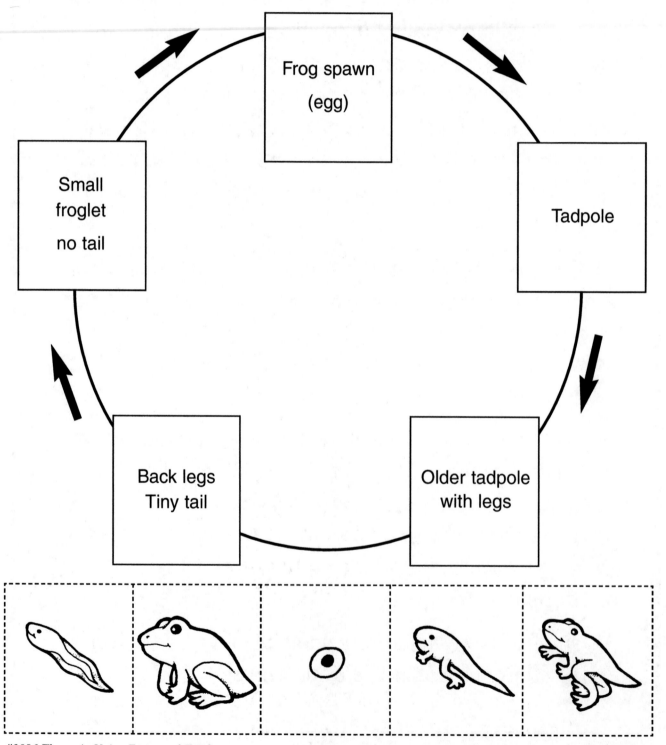

Frog and Toad Art Projects

Paper Plate Frog

Materials
- small white paper plates (dessert size)
- green tempera paint
- green construction paper (9" x 12" or 23 cm x 30 cm)
- scraps of black, white, and red or pink construction paper

Directions
1. Each student needs to paint the front and back sides of a paper plate with the green tempera paint. Let the plates dry thoroughly.
2. Have children cut the green construction paper into four strips. Older children can measure their papers into four strips that are three inches (8 cm) wide. Cut a "V" section into one end of each strip to make them look more like frogs' feet. Fan-fold the legs to give them some "spring" action.
3. Students then fold their paper plates in half. Have them glue two of the legs onto the back of the plate (where the fold is) and two of the strips off to the sides.
4. Students use the black and white construction paper to make big eyes for the frog. They need to make a small fold at the bottom of each eye and apply glue there. Children attach the eyes to the top of the paper plate. The eyes should "pop" up.
5. Each child cuts a strip of red construction paper into a long, thin strip. This will be the frog's tongue. Students fan-fold the tongue and glue it inside the paper plate. The tongue should look like it is sticking out of the frog's mouth.

Tissue Paper Polliwog

Materials
- white construction paper (12" x 18" or 30 cm x 46 cm)
- various shades of blue and green tissue paper
- starch
- black tempera paint
- paintbrushes

Directions
1. Distribute a piece of white construction paper to each child.
2. The students rip the tissue paper into long strips.
3. Then lay strips of tissue paper onto the construction paper; paint over it with starch.
4. Let the paper dry thoroughly.
5. Students trim any excess tissue from the edges of the construction paper.
6. Students use the black tempera paint to paint the silhouettes of tadpoles onto the tissue-covered construction paper.

Frog and Toad Art Projects *(cont.)*

Froggy Pop-Up Puppet

Materials

- Styrofoam cup for each student
- pencils
- frog pattern (see below)
- Easter grass
- google eyes
- glue

Directions

1. Color the frog pattern below and then cut it out. Attach some google eyes with glue.

2. Glue the frog to the end of a pencil. Insert the pencil into a cup by piercing a hole into the bottom of the cup.

3. Fill the cup with colorful Easter grass.

4. Make your puppet jump by moving the pencil up and down through the hole.

Extension

You can put on a short play or act out a scene with a classmate by using your frog puppets.

Frog and Toad Art Projects *(cont.)*

Papier-Mâché Frog or Toad

Teacher Note: *Prepare the papier-mâché glue from any standard classroom recipe before beginning this activity.*

Materials

- lots of newspaper
- masking tape
- papier-mâché recipe
- paint
- scissors
- assorted materials to add details

Directions

1. Form the shape of your animal by crumpling sheets of newspaper into tight wads.
2. Using masking tape, tape the wads together to make a basic shape of a frog or toad.
3. Cover the animal with several layers of papier-mâché.
4. When the animal form is completely dry, paint the animal its natural color. Add any details that would make your papier-mâché frog or toad more realistic.

Frog and Toad Story Masks

Materials

- poster board or heavy cardstock paper
- thin elastic or string
- hole punch
- scissors
- markers, crayons, and/or paints

Directions

1. Using a pencil, draw a frog pattern (an example is shown on the right) onto a piece of poster board or heavy cardstock.
2. Color and decorate the mask as you wish. Add appropriate details.
3. Cut out the pattern and then carefully cut out the eyes.

4. Punch holes at the sides and attach a length of elastic or tape a tongue depressor at the side of the mask and hold it in front of your eyes.

Create a Classroom Frog Life Cycle Book

Directions

1. Have students create an Eric Carle classroom book about the life cycle of a frog. First, bring Eric Carle's books to class and show the artwork (a great one to start with is *The Very Hungry Caterpillar*). Get students excited by telling them that they can make one too. This is a two-day activity.

2. The first day give each student a large sheet of fingerpainting glossy paper. If you don't have any, the best thing to use is the back of posters. Have students completely cover the page with one color of fingerpaint. Give all students a different color so that there will be a variety. Let the pages dry completely.

3. On the second day, divide the students into groups and assign each group a stage of the life cycle. Give each group a large sheet of white construction paper (11" x 16" or 28 cm x 41 cm). Have them work as a group, cutting out shapes from the fingerpainted pages and gluing them onto the white paper to represent their life cycle stage. Do not let students draw on the pages.

4. After students have finished their stage of the life cycle, brainstorm together what the story line should be. They could make up a cute story about a particular tadpole and give him a name and follow him through all the stages.

5. After the words have been added, laminate the pages so they are smooth surfaces and bind them together in order. When complete, the classroom book should look like an Eric Carle book.

Un-frog-get-able Activities

Use this tic-tac-toe sheet to choose any three activities to celebrate frogs and toads.

After your projects are complete, share your work with others.

1	2	3
A statue is being dedicated to honor Frog and Toad's friendship. You are the honored speaker at the ceremony. Write a speech for this celebration.	Draw a cartoon about two old frogs in a pond. Write a funny caption.	Read *The Yellow Brick Toad* and write a silly story, riddle, or cartoon to add to the book.
4 After reading *The Mysterious Tadpole*, write about a mysterious tadpole found in your backyard.	**5** Write an acrostic poem for F R O G S	**6** If you could be any kind of frog or toad, what kind would you be? Why? E-mail your teacher with your answer.
7 Design a three-page electronic slide show presentation to show what you have learned about frogs and toads.	**8** Write a different ending to *The Frog Prince* or *The Frog Prince Continued*.	**9** Pretend you are a frog and describe the world from your point of view.

Lily Pad Time
Bulletin Board Game

Directions: Create a bulletin board math game called Lily Pad Time. You will need a die, frog pieces, clocks, and bulletin board paper with lily pads cut from construction paper attached. (Depending on whether you have the game on the floor or on the wall, you can use Velcro to stick the frogs to the lily pads. If you have a magnetic chalkboard, use magnets.) Have lily pads leading from start to finish. Students must roll the die and advance their frog on the lily pads the correct number of spaces. Each lily pad should have a time written on it. As a student lands on a lily pad, that student sets the clock to the time that is written. If the student sets the time correctly, that player gets to stay on the space. If students do not set the time correctly, they must go back to their previous space. The game ends when all students have crossed the pond to the finish line. This game could easily be adapted for phonics by putting certain sounds on each lily pad (for example: ar). Students will have to say a word that has that sound (like "car"). It could also be used for addition and subtraction drills.

Lily Pad Time
Bulletin Board Game *(cont.)*

Directions: Each student should color and cut out a frog pattern for the game.

Frog Bookmarks

74

Frog Stationery

Awards

Student's Name

receives this award for

un-frog-getable

good work

Teacher's Signature

Toad-a-ly Awesome

Student Award

presented to

Student's Name

Teacher's Signature

Multimedia

Here is a list of some software, Web sites, sound cassettes, videos, and manipulatives that you might want to incorporate into your frog and toad unit lesson plans.

Computer Software

Destination Rain Forest. Available from Crimson Multimedia Distribution, Inc. Students step into a Panamanian rain forest, where they participate in interactive learning about exotic plants, insects, waterfalls, and Kuna Indians. Students select scenes and characters, plan plots, write, narrate, animate, and record dialogue on this adventure.

Magic School Bus Explores the Rainforest. Available from Crimson Multimedia Destribution, Inc. Students explore the Costa Rican Rain Forest with Ms. Frizzle while learning important science concepts.

The Pond. Available from Sunburst. Using the pond environment, students learn to organize information, uncover patterns, and describe patterns.

Zurk's Rainforest Lab. Available from Sunburst. Five activities build a foundation for learning in life science and mathematics developing critical thinking skills.

Web Sites

Belize Zoo. *www.belizezoo.org/zoo/zoo/herps/fro/fro1.html*

The Frog Pages. *http://www.geocities.com/TheTropics/1337*

Frogland. *http://www.allaboutfrogs.org/froglnd.shtml*

Rainforest Australia - Rainforest Frogs. *http://www.rainforest-australia.com/frogs.htm*

Sound Cassettes

Kellogg, Steven. *Mysterious Tadpole.* Dial, 1977.

Langstaff, John. *Songs for Singing Children.* Revel Records, 1996.

Lobel, Arnold. *Frog and Toad Are Friends Kit.* Harper and Row, 1970.

Videos

A Boy, a Dog and a Frog. Videotape. Goodtimes Home Video, 1995. 30 minutes.

Eyewitness Amphibian. Videotape. DK Vision, 1996. 35 minutes.

Eyewitness Pond & River. Videotape. DK Vision, 1996. 35 minutes.

Frog Goes to Dinner. Videotape. Phoenix Films and Video, 1992. 12 minutes.

Manipulatives

Evolving Tadpole Set. Polyurethane set features 4 stages of development. Available from Insect Lore.

Frog Hatchery Kit. Includes a coupon for tadpoles along with an aquarium, magnifying glass, instruction booklet, and food. Available from Insect Lore.

Frog Metamorphosis Stamp Set. Set of 6 stamps. Available from Insect Lore.

Pond Life Puzzle. Features 48 jumbo pieces. Available from Insect Lore.

Red-Eyed Tree Frog Puzzle. Measures 3' x 2' (91 cm x 61 cm). Available from Insect Lore.

Surf Frogs—A Live Frog Growing Habitat. Includes a 17" long habitat with frog coupons. Available from Insect Lore.

Annotated Bibliography

Bernstein, Joanne E. *Un-frog-gettable Riddles*. Whitman, 1981.
A collection of frog riddles.

Billings, Charlene. *Spring Peepers Are Calling*. Dodd, 1978.
Discusses the life cycle of the spring peeper and the capture and care of this tiny frog as a pet.

Blake, Quentin. *Story of the Dancing Frog*. Knopf, 1985.
Follows the ups and downs of Great Aunt Gertrude and her lively companion, George the frog, as they dance their way around the world to gain fame and fortune.

Chinery, Michael. *Frog*. Troll, 1991.
An introduction to the life cycle of a frog.

Cole, Joanna. *A Frog's Body*. William Morrow, 1980.
Close-up photographs and text explain the details of a frog's anatomy.

Cowley, Joy. *Red Eyed Tree Frog*. Scholastic, 1999.
This frog found in the rain forest of Central America spends the night searching for food while also being careful not to become dinner for some other animal.

Dallinger, Jane. *Frogs and Toads*. Lerner Publications, 1982.
Text and photographs describe the transformation of tadpoles into mature frogs and toads.

Hazen, Barbara Shook. *That Toad Is Mine*. Harper Collins, 1998.
Two friends like to share everything, but when they find a toad and argue over how to share it, they eventually leave it to its own environment.

Henwood, Chris. *Frogs*. Watts, 1988.
Describes the characteristics and behavior of frogs, looks at their life cycle, and explains how to create a terrarium.

Hogan, Paula. *The Frog*. Raintree, 1979.
Explains in simple terms the life cycle of a frog.

Hogner, Dorothy. *Frogs and Polliwogs*. Thomas Y. Crowell, 1956.
Carefully describes both frogs and tadpoles and shows unique characteristics of each.

Jeunesse, Gallimard and Daniel Moignot. *Frogs—A First Discovery Book*. Scholastic, 1994.
Introduces the life cycle, habitat, species, and activity of frogs.

Kalan, Robert. *Jump, Frog, Jump*. Greenwillow, 1981.
A cumulative tale in which a frog tries to catch a fly without getting caught itself.

Kellogg, Steven. *The Mysterious Tadpole*. Dial, 1977.
It soon becomes clear that Louis's pet tadpole is not turning into an ordinary frog.

Langstaff, J. *Frog Went a Courtin'*. Harcourt, 1991.
Illustrates the well-known American folk song about the courtship and marriage of the frog and mouse.

Lionni, Leo. *It's Mine!* Knopf, 1986.
Three selfish frogs quarrel over who owns their pond and island until a storm makes them value the benefits of sharing.

Lobel, Arnold. *Frog and Toad Are Friends*. Harper & Row, 1970.
A frog and toad's everyday adventure in friendship.

Macdonald, Fiona. *Rain Forest*. Raintree Steck-Vaughn, 1994.
Gives information about various lives in the rain forest.

Annotated Bibliography (cont.)

Mayer, Mercer. *Frog Goes to Dinner*. Puffin Books, 1992.
  Having stowed away in a pocket, Frog wreaks havoc and creates disgrace for the family at the posh restaurant where they are having dinner.

Mayer, Mercer. *Frog, Where Are You?* Dial Books Young, 1980.
  Chronicles the humorous adventures that befall a young boy as he and his dog search for the frog that escaped from a jar in his room.

Morris, Dean. *Frogs and Toads*. Raintree, 1988.
  An introduction to various frogs and toads, their physical characteristics, and behavior.

Naden, Corinne. *Let's Find Out About Frogs*. Watts, 1972.
  An easy-to-read description of the physical characteristics and behavior of frogs.

Patent, Dorothy Hinshaw. *Flashy Fantastic Rain Forest Frogs*. Walker and Co., 1997.
  Describes the physical characteristics, behavior, reproduction, and habitat of frogs that live in the rain forest.

Pfeffer, Wendy. *From Tadpole to Frog*. Harper Collins, 1994.
  Describes the metamorphosis from tadpole to frog.

Porte, Barbara Ann. *Tale of a Tadpole*. Orchard, 1997.
  Francine and her family watch as their pet tadpole, Fred, gradually changes into what they think is a frog until Grandpa tells them Fred is a toad that should be living in the backyard.

Pratt, Kristin Joy. *A Walk in the Rainforest*. Dawn Publications, 1992.
  A sampling of living things in the rain forest.

Pursell, Margaret. *Sprig the Tree Frog*. Carolrhoda, 1976.
  A boy takes home a mass of tree frog eggs from a pond, protects them, raises them, and eventually returns them to their natural home.

Scieszka, Jon. *The Frog Prince Continued*. Puffin, 1991.
  After the frog turns into a prince, he and the princess do not live happily ever after, and the Prince decides to look for a witch to help him remedy the situation.

Simon, Seymour. *Discovering What Frogs and Toads Do*. McGraw, 1969.
  Describes the habits and habitats of frogs, their maturation process, and their anatomy. Includes instructions on starting and maintaining an aquarium.

Tarcov, E. *Frog Prince*. Four Winds Press, 1974.
  Angry at being forced to keep her promise to a frog, the princess finally resorts to violent action with unexpected results.

Taylor, Barbara. *Rain Forest*. Covent Garden Books Ltd., 1998.
  Gives descriptions and background information about the rain forest.

Teague, Mark. *Frog Medicine*. Scholastic, 1991.
  When Elmo was assigned to read a book about frog medicine by his teacher, he began to experience strange symptoms which warranted the need for a frog doctor.

Thaler, Mike. *The Yellow Brick Toad: Funny Frog Cartoons, Riddles and Silly Stories*. Doubleday, 1978.
  Jokes, riddles, cartoons, and funny stories concerning frogs and toads.

Wiesner, David. *Tuesday*. Clarion, 1991.
  Frogs rise on their lily pads, float through the air, and explore nearby houses while their inhabitants sleep.

Answer Key

Page 14
1. $3 + 4 = 7$
2. $4 - 3 = 1$
3. $4 + 5 = 9$
4. $5 + 1 = 6$
5. $6 + 4 = 10$

Pages 28–30
The red eyed tree frog won't eat katydids.

The red eyed tree frog will eat moths.

The red eyed tree frog won't eat ants.

The red eyed tree frog won't eat caterpillars.

The red eyed tree frog won't eat iguanas.

Page 33
1. sticky feet
2. eardrum
3. eyes
4. mouth
5. expandable throat

Page 37
1. Agalychnis
2. nocturnal
3. Central
4. carnivores
5. eggs
6. suction
7. rain forest
8. deforestation
9. Hylidae
10. startle coloration

Page 47
8:00 P.M., 9:00 P.M., 11:00 P.M., 12:00 A.M., 1:00 A.M., 3:00 A.M., 4:00 A.M., 5:00 A.M., 7:00 A.M., 8:00 A.M.

Page 54

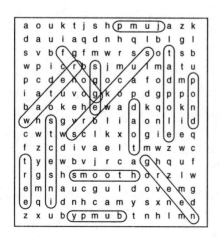

Page 55
Answers will vary.

Page 56
1. red eyed tree frog
2. gills
3. tadpole
4. skin
5. insects

Page 57
1. 49
2. 25
3. 67
4. 37
5. 76
6. 88
7. 94
8. 40
9. 59
10. 44

Page 58
Answers will vary.

Page 62
1. The daylights hours and temperature increase.

2. The pond animals grow and become more active. The plants begin to grow.

3. Tadpoles and other small animals eat plants. They are herbivores. Small meat eaters eat the herbivores. They are carnivores. The small carnivores then become food for the larger meat eaters.

4. The remains of plants and animals provide food and minerals for other pond plants and animals.

5. Some pond animals lay eggs, and some fatten up in anticipation of winter. Pond plants are drying out and beginning to die.

6. It is easier to find food because it is more abundant in the spring.

7. Answers will vary.

8. Answers will vary.

Page 64
Answers will vary.